Ellipsism

Alex Zivic

Ellipsism
copyright © 2020 by Alex Zivic. All rights reserved.
Manufactured in the United States of America. No part of this
publication may be reproduced, stored in any
retrieval system, or transmitted in any form or by any means,
mechanical, photocopying, recording, or otherwise, without
permission in writing from the publisher.

Publishing Concepts, LLC
6590 Scanlan Ave., St. Louis, MO 63139

PublishingConceptsLLC.com

ISBN: 9798690850753
Library of Congress Control Number: 2020917823

Lead Editor and Designer: Emily Klein
Cover and Page Art: @wafalo

ellipsism.org

For bulk/wholesale orders, please contact Publishing
Concepts, LLC at (314) 781-8880.

Proceeds from *Ellipsism* directly benefit ALIVE St. Louis.

My name is Alex Zivic
Thank you for reading Ellipsism.

Alternatives to Living in Violent Environments (ALIVE) empowers St. Louis area families impacted by domestic abuse. The nonprofit agency's mission is to provide counseling, emergency sanctuary, and other critical services to adults and children impacted by domestic abuse.

Services are available to all domestic violence survivors, regardless of gender identity, gender expression, sexual orientation, race, religion, ability, age, or socioeconomic means. ALIVE's offices and shelter locations are fully accessible, and resources are available to accommodate individuals with special needs. Services are free to clients, and no one is ever turned away due to inability to pay. Over 80% of ALIVE clients represent underserved populations.

Please visit www.alivestl.org for more information or to help. Thank you for supporting ALIVE's vision to end domestic abuse, restoring safety and peace one family at a time.

Ellipsism
A Vision
And then it fades
Vanishing, like the end of days

Ellipsism n.
A sense of sadness experienced by the realization
that one won't live to see the future.
Never knowing how history will turn out,
but knowing you're a part of it.

Give or take,
It's hard to define a feeling

Begin –
It calls
I look
I've lost
My mind
I see
It lurks
Down in
The Void
It's Not Alive
But It Exists
It's Part Of Me
I'm Part Of It
I wait
It knows
I bet
It folds
I fight
It wins
For now,
But then
I Find
My mind
Down in
The Void

I hope I don't fall in
Begin –

I hope I don't fall In
Begin –

Visions
It comes to me in visions
It comes to me in visions
(visions)
Now I, oh I, can see it
And now I don't know
what to believe in

So I
let go —
instead,
Let it take hold
release the mind
become the host
alternate state
beyond the void

And as
the vessel
comes to light —
Now you can see it,
so do I

The Concept of Why
Ellipsism is my abstract comprehension of existence.
A state of being, in-between, seemingly knowing the end
before it begins — or the beginning of the end.
Visions of a paradox. Visions of us.
Nothing lasts forever
But right now
It's real

Why?
I'd often ask
Why do we love?
Why do we live just to die?
And if we've already know the ending, then why?

Concepts without a definitive answer
And nobody really knows, aside
from their interpretation of the concept of Why.

I've tried to understand and comprehend it, as best I can.
And I've learned that we are all capable of finding our own
narratives for these concepts. We define our reason to live —
which is a wonderful thing, until you're unwilling to accept the
consequences of a false narrative.

I thought I knew everything about Ellipsism.
And above all, I've learned that I know nothing.
That some things are simply out of our control, no matter how
much we may manifest the outcome.
Unfortunately, we may never know the answers
to such abstract comprehensions

Therefore, of course, we live only to die.
We love, without understanding the concept of why.

It's all beyond comprehension,
but we all try to understand it.
What a beautiful thing.

And the rest,
there's absolutely nothing
we can do about it —
unless you force a narrative
and then hope for the best

To foresee the end before it begins
Is no different than to ignore the signs

The heart is a figment of the mind

I can only offer what I am
and who I want to be
Love me

The Beach and Me
We sit and think
sometimes of love
or idle things

the ocean sings
she doesn't speak
I understand
She waves at me

Together, here
We share our thoughts
write in the sand
our secrets lost

At times we laugh
And others cry
together still
beneath the sky

Under the sun
we soak its rays
we even talk
on cloudy days

under the moon
we pray together
for broken hearts
or better weather

Sometimes I leave
for months or weeks
She waits for me
asleep at sea

But I come back
and so does she
We sit and think
the beach and me.

West Palm

Sundown, hair is bleach-dyed
Your fingers trace my tan lines
We kiss, I lick your lip balm
I fell for you in West Palm

Although we're shallow near the surface
Along the depths I know we're hurting
A Friend I never knew I needed
Under the ocean, coral bleaches

Waves
Crash into me
When I crash into you

Infinity

I don't think I've ever known real romance.
But I know what it feels like to wish the
days away,

With you

They seemed endless
I was wrong.

That felt real to me

Eyes
They can't see anything
Visions, nor premonitions
They can't see the truth
But I do

.

Visions
—ideas, concepts, perceptions—
Theories deep in thought. of anything. of us.

They visit me at night, or anytime. When I'm alone.
On a long walk. Or at the beach.
With or without you.

Visions are my interpretations.
Not always of what I intend to see,
but they are what I've envisioned.

Sometimes a complete narrative
Others, just a word.

And over time,
I've pieced together the perceptions
that make the most sense—
Until they make sense to me.

And most importantly,
As much as I may manifest a vision,
It will not always come true.

Whatever we are now stems from my own delusion

Pull
body and mind
stretched to their limits
from a heart that's pulled apart

I sank into the depths
Trying to drown out every word
That would keep me away from you

The beginning or the end
doesn't matter that much.

I've been fixated on the feeling in-between,
when you know it's not working out
but you keep trying anyway.

I know it's time to go,
But I won't

I put it off
To the beach
To paradise.
At least, that's what I pretend it feels like

Nothing lasts forever
I understand, and that's ok

This explodes if you drop it

shards of heart,
they cut like shrapnel
from every broken moment
pieced back together
until finally,
it broke.

Ellipsism

I know. I think I've always known. You and I were not meant to be. But I often ask myself *why*. Why did we spend countless days and nights trying to make us work when we both knew it wasn't going to end well? ? I wonder how much sleep I lost while trying to find the answers. And I'd daydream of scenes that never existed while trying to figure it out. I saw visions of what could be. I thought I envisioned the perfect future for us. What happened? It doesn't make any sense. I suppose you could try to simplify it and just say that everything happens for a reason, but even I don't believe that. Could you see what I could see? Did we ever see the same things? What am I to you? And if you knew, then why would you show me that version of you? I'm still learning to accept the truth. You hurt me. And I hurt you. And I don't understand why. I know I'll never know. I'm now focused on the parts of me that I can still control. This is how I feel.

It might not be right, but it's real.

Nih

You can imagine —
But you can't see until you lose a loved one.
Everything that mattered before, means nothing now.
And what seemed like nothing then, is now everything.

I want it in my veins, somehow

The allure of temptation is the
ability to resist it
But I really, really miss you.

Some days, you weigh heavy on my mind
And it drags me back down into the depths

I can still see the surface
We must not be that deep

It was
A shot in the dark,
but I hit it

No, we can't just. be. friends.
I'd rather be alone. than. this.

If lightning never strikes twice,
I thought you'd be the one
to save us

See through the guise
Fall for my mind

I don't need eyes
to see the vision

I see it
when my eyes are closed

Some days
when you look at me

I know your eyes
are closed.

Beyond

You look into my eyes
But you can't see me.

Why can't you see me?

Another day goes by without it
I'm starting to forget (,) I want it

I'm starting to forget (,) I want it

Solemn

They knelt,
Pleading with the sea,

"Heaven, help me."

And the waves whispered back,

"Save yourself."

Forgive me,

In trying to make sense of it all
I'd forgotten that you are healing, too.

Your scars were deeper than mine.
I hope you don't sink as far as I did.

Statue
Be Still
Watch

It was my first thought in the morning,
and my last before I'd fall asleep.

It was when those days and nights started to blend together
that I realized I had a problem.

I was still thinking of you.
You'd already forgotten about me.

I tried to self-medicate, all of it

It didn't work.
It just made things worse.

I couldn't sleep

I fell

into

an

endless

cycle

I made bad habits. And even worse decisions.

existence is fragile

I ask,
As aches become numb
And my senses fade —
where am I going?
will I be ok?

I feel like I can't breathe
And I can't feel my limbs
In that moment I realize
this might be the end

That pill
felt so heavy
I don't want to be dead
But after that last pill
there's no sound from the bed

I didn't mean to do it
I hope they don't think that I tried
And I,

I know, I have a past
But I — I'm already over that

It's too late to leave a note,
I know you wouldn't read it though

I know I've made mistakes, but I —
I know there's more than this
Please, give me another chance —
Then I wake up in the abyss.

absence of time right now
silence

I open my eyes in the void.
Before me lies en entity, as omniscient as the light,
but as vast as the dark itself.
And then it takes my form,
It mirrors me

It tosses what appears to be
a representation of my mind,
back and forth, between grave hands,
like an apple from the tree.
And it looks up to ask me —
Why?

In awe,
I think for a moment
that it doesn't know.
And then I answer —

I don't know
It looks me up and down for a moment and
returns its gaze upon the mind.

I think you know,
It whispers,
But I don't,
I decline.

I thought I saw the vision,
But all I see is you

And then it stops, it cracks a smile,
and it locks its eyes with mine,
and says —
I know you saw the vision

I say —
Then why do you ask why?

It says —
We both see the same vision,
but I know you're not ready to die

I think,
I feign a laugh —
It knows I can

You are me?
I ask
And this time
the being laughs

Yes, but you already knew that —
hand clenched around the object

Then why do you have my mind?
I ask

The heart is an aspect of the mind,
It says, as it points to where its heart should be

Then I look down,
I see it now
in the dark
I am the keeper of the heart

You and I
The heart, the mind
We have the exact same eyes.

But we don't always see the same things.

I pause —
I wait a moment.
I know exactly what it means.

Not all visions
in the void
are what I'd hoped to see.

I thought I knew,
I saw the vision

But not in its entirety...

In place of pain
You kept the heart
For that's all that you could see —
you shunned the mind
You took it off
And you gave that part to me.

I ask,
If I can see
What you can see,
Then why can't they
see you & me?

I know you love them,
Answers the void.
That's why you
must set them free.

I hold my breath,
I nod my head,
then finally, I agree.

Now you get it,
laughs the void —
as it extends it's arm to me —

Our eyes lock
I reach the mind
And it becomes a part of me.

The void
is the vision
of what I don't want to see.

Together now,
heart and mind—
I see the vision,
now I'm looking out for me.

I know that I know nothing
But I'm learning every day

A paradisal paradox
It makes sense,
but also not

*we make sense,
but also not*

After all,
I've taught myself
that fear will pass
like any storm
of sadness
or self-doubt.

And when I find
that's not enough
I remember
why you left me here.
I couldn't see
what you could see,
but now I see it clear.

I've
harnessed
visions
in the void.
I control
my heart
and mind

here

Minimal. Less.

Sigh of relief — which has a name,

Ellipsism

I don't wanna let go
I don't wanna be here alone

And I really wish you love
that's all I want
that's all I know

I promise after all
we'll both be
better off
alone

I don't know where or when right now
We've reached the end,
Goodbye for now

I first, I wasn't sure
And I know it's gonna hurt
But after time,
I've seen the signs
I think I've known

And now it's time.
I know you know
I wish you love

Like you,
My past will be a part of me.
I'm not that person anymore

It's part of me
I'm part of it

My mind and self
We are aspects of the heart
Together, we are healing
May we never mend apart

Virga

Her name
was written in the rain
She swore she'd never fall again
Then left me standing in the street

I begged you not to go, but
You were always meant to leave
And I may never understand it
But maybe we're not meant to, Be(a)

I loved you
All the same
She never left
Now fall like rain

As the beauty
in the black dress,
and you will know
her name

Virga: noun
: wisps of rain appearing to hang under a cloud and evaporating before reaching the ground.
"the ghostly apparition of virga — an indicator of violent downdrafts"

I thought I loved you,
But I don't remember your beautiful, blue eyes
Or the way they blended away with the waves.

But I fall,
deep into his endless, abyssal eyes
Even when mine are closed.

If you let go — I will catch you

Presence
I am alive
I can walk
I can talk
I can hear
I can see
I can be anything
I want to be
I have skin
I have eyes
I have fingers
I have bones
I can visit places
I want to go
I can think
I can write
I can draw
I can read
I can feel
I can love
I can be
I am free

It's a late night
in the city
the park is empty
I'm here alone
and I can see it

Visions
and views
I never shared with you
like nothing ever happened,
but I swear I wanted to

I close my eyes
You're not here —
I'm by myself, tonight
At first I start to miss you
But I really don't tonight.

Reflection

Sometimes it doesn't hit me until I'm standing in the mirror with someone else. You are gone.

I'm learning to look into the mirror
to see myself.

Some days
I start to miss us
But we're never alone
At Francis

In finding you
I found myself
I saw the vision
I wrote

Ellipsism

You are gone.
And I am still here.

Acceptance

You were idealizing an idea
that you didn't understand.
And once you accept
That you don't know
Why
Things happened
the way they did
It's a lot easier
to understand,
or comprehend
that you
deserve
better

I think I know
But then I don't

Lately I've been sleeping
resting when my eyes are closed

It's crazy, isn't it?

In the midst of our own undoing,
that's where we learn.

It's tangible pain.

How beautiful.
How cruel.

Tonight, I look better in the dark

Looking back, I should have let go a long time ago.

But it happened.
I learned from it.

And I've also come to the realization that I held on for so long because I was afraid I'd never find another love like ours.

Maybe that's a good thing.

I met someone new today.

It won't work out,
but we locked eyes and I looked away when he told me mine were beautiful. I said thank you. I meant it.

I forgot what that felt like.

I do have beautiful eyes.

To say what can't be said
To tear visions apart
That's it
That's art.

Eternity

I am who I am
And everything
I couldn't see
You saw,
And you loved me for me

Safeguard my heart
Please keep it safe
You kept it
When you walked away

Someday, I know
You'll give it back
When I meet you
At the end of days

I promise you
I'll find a way
To see
What you could see —

In your eyes,
I saw a vision
Now you're watching
Over me

Forever
Is a long time
Yes. I am afraid.
One day we will all share
In that exact the same fate.

We are all one in the same
But you are you
And I am I
Why

Nobody knows

We are predestined
to live a fate we can't explain
By means of faith, or other ways
Not by beliefs, or religion
it is truth
Until then, I ask of you

Find meaning in your convictions
In your
Visions
And see them through.

Thank you for reading Ellipsism.

When it's my time to go,
Will I know?

Will this matter after all?
Cause this is all I've ever known

And I'm trying
to comprehend
why
love & death
share the same tones.

At least we live
It kind of hurts,
But at least we're not alone.

After all,
This is all we have

An answer
I'm thankful
That I know

All of the gods
have their names
signed into the stars

— Why don't you?
— Why can't I?

Now this is mine

Let these words
stand as testament

That I was here.
Written in your mind.
Etched into your heart, forever.

In waiting for the perfect moment
of that which will never be
remind yourself
to find freedom
in the now
find your
release

If these words never reach you
I hope that someone does in time
Nothing lasts forever, but right now

(You are worth it)
(You are loved)
(You are here)
 You are alive

Ellipsism
A Vision
And then it fades
Vanishing, like the end of days

Nothing lasts forever
I understand, and that's ok
I know that I know nothing
But I'm learning every day

—

*I hope I don't fall in
Begin —*

*— Nothing lasts forever,
but forever has no end*

Ellipsism by Alex Zivic

@WAFALO

Thank you for illustrating my visions.
Your talent is beyond words, and it shows through your art.
I couldn't have done it without you.

Emily Klein
@emsdrawings.jpg

We made a book!
You helped form Ellipsism into the project that exists today.
Thank you for your time, talent, and for being my dear friend.

INDEX

Intro – 1
Definition – 3
Begin – 5
Visions – 9
The Concept of Why – 11
Foresee the End – 14
The Heart Is a Figment of the Mind – 15
Offer – 17
The Beach & Me – 18
West Palm – 20
Coral – 23
Crash – 24
Infinity – 27
Nor – 29
—Visions— 31
Delusion – 33
Pull – 37
Depths – 39
Paradise – 40
Nothing – 43
This Explodes If You Drop It – 45
Shards of Heart – 46
Ellipsism — Full –49
Nih – 51
I Want It in My Veins, Somehow – 53
Allure – 54
Surface – 55
Hit – 56
Alone – 59
Lightning – 60
Guise – 63
Closed – 64
Beyond – 65
Another Day Goes By Without It – 66
I'm Starting To Forget (,) I Want It – 67
Solemn – 68
Sink – 71

Statue – 72
Cycle – 74
Habits – 75
Existence Is Fragile – 77
Will I Be Ok? – 79
Silence – 81
The Heart & Mind – 82
I Know That I Know Nothing – 89
Paradisal Paradox – 91
Here – 93
Minimal. Less. – 94
Sigh of Relief — Which Has a Name – 97
I Wish You Love – 99
It's Part of Me — I'm Part of It – 101
Aspects – 102
Virga – 104
Abyssal – 107
If You Let Go—I Will Catch You – 109
Presence – 111
Late – 112
Reflection – 115
Francis – 116
I Wrote – 117
You Are Gone – 119
Acceptance – 120
I Think I Know – 123
Cruel – 125
Tonight, I Look Better in the Dark – 127
I Do – 129
Art – 131
Eternity – 133
Forever – 135
Will I Know? – 136
Now This Is Mine – 138
Etched – 141
Release – 145
Alive – 146
Ellipsism – 149

www.ellipsism.org

Made in the USA
Monee, IL
02 October 2020